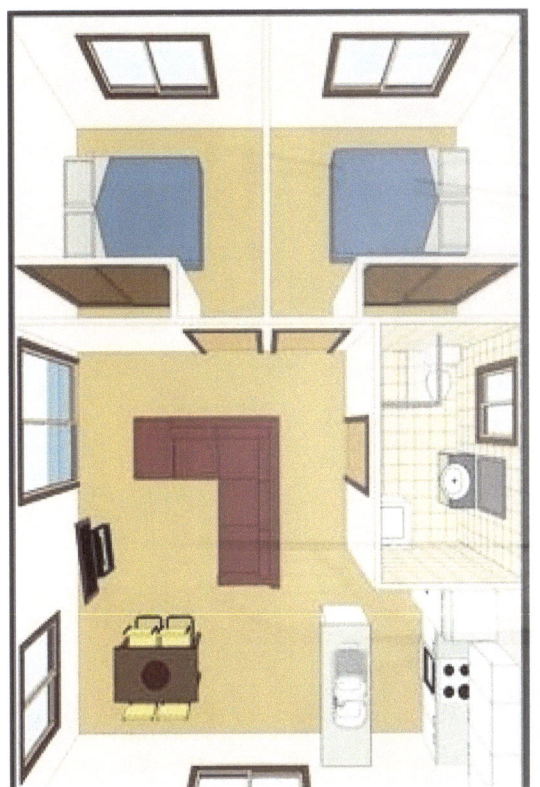

GRANNY FLATS
MINI GUIDES 2016

BRIAN RIDER   Full Colour

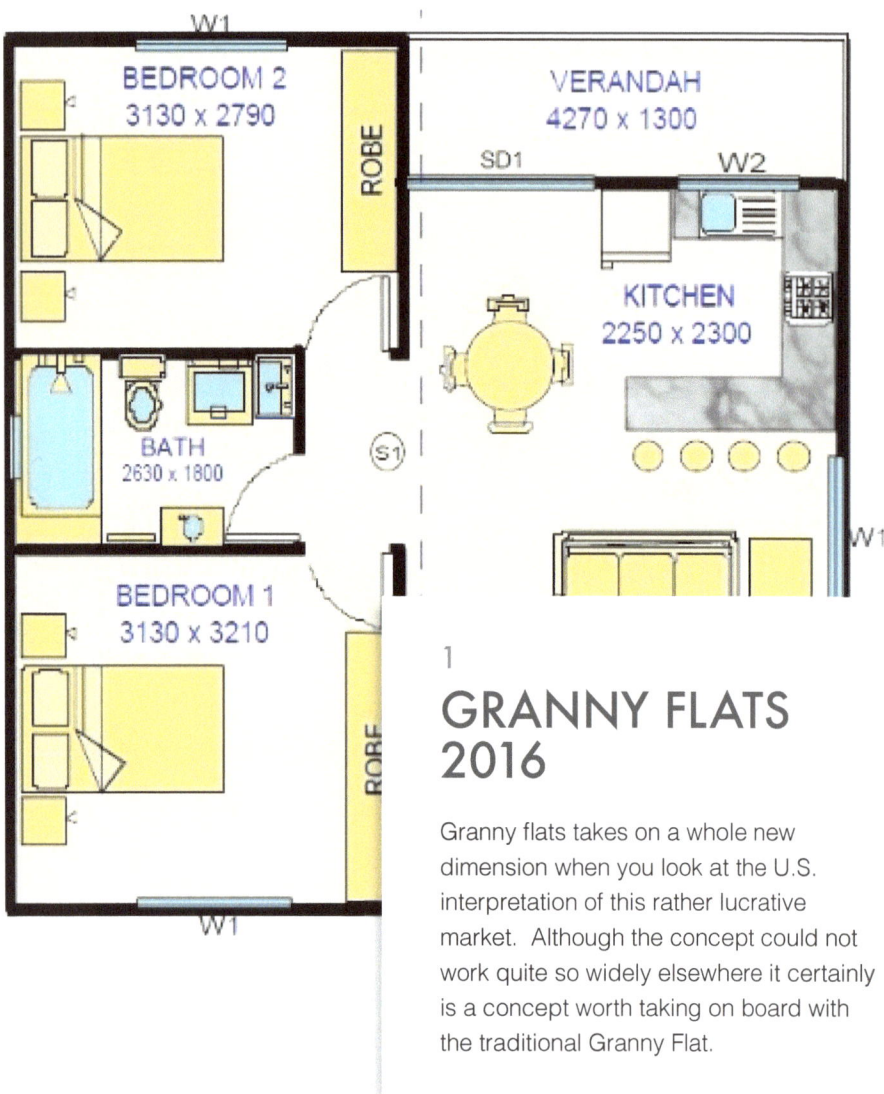

1

GRANNY FLATS 2016

Granny flats takes on a whole new dimension when you look at the U.S. interpretation of this rather lucrative market. Although the concept could not work quite so widely elsewhere it certainly is a concept worth taking on board with the traditional Granny Flat.

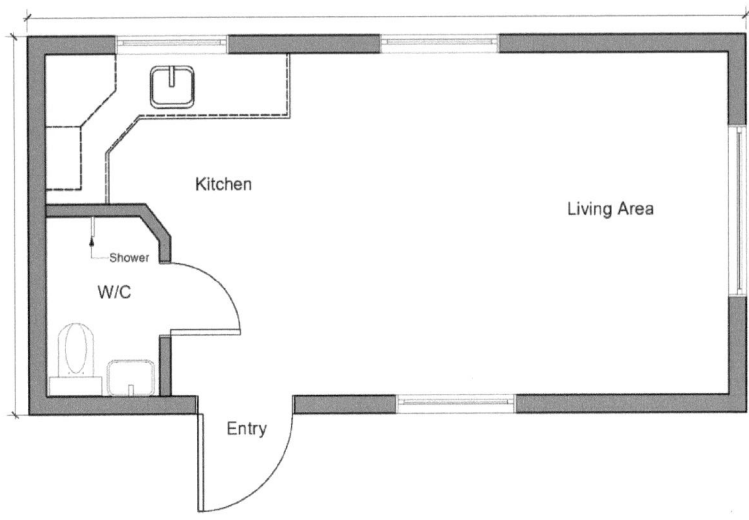

The floor plan shows: Kitchen, Living Area, Shower, W/C, and Entry.

WHAT IS AN ACCEPTABLE GRANNY FLAT?

1. Self contained with separate entrance.

2. Probably best on ground level on one floor.

3. Make sure sufficient safety features are installed such as grab rails and adjustable beds.

4. User friendly seating and sufficient space for entertaining.

5. Properly designed kitchen facility

I think the word 'acceptable' is an important one. There is no good cramming the elderly lady into a confined space. Care should be taken to ensure that the most comfortable facility possible is being constructed for the lady or gentleman to comfortably see out their declining years. Also remember that older people have a high incidence of dementia in one form or another so that regular attended care will be necessary. Also remember not only the cost of a care home but the entire, often repulsive, concept of a care home.

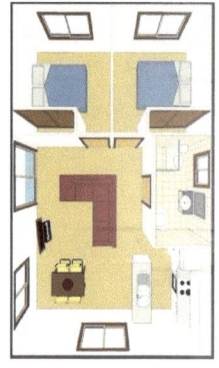

The Contemporary

60 m2

GRANNY FLAT DESIGN

What does the term Granny Flat mean to you? In the States it is big business and it is not a flat in the conventional sense it is a freestanding building and they get top dollar.

So why are we focusing on this subject this in this book. With our own experience it is clear that many people could benefit from a design service that specialises in designing conversion for Granny Flats, especially with the cost of care homes these days

THE AMERICAN GRANNY FLAT

THE AVERAGE GRANNY FLAT

1. One or two bedrooms

2. Bathroom or shower-room

3. And, usually. a combined kitchen living area

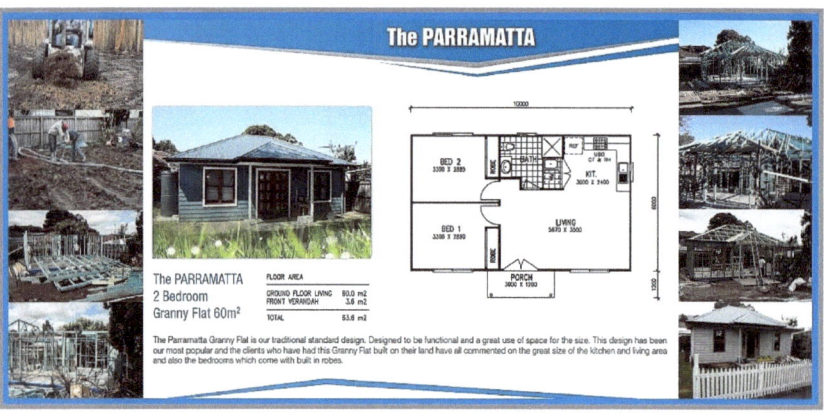

The PARRAMATTA

The PARRAMATTA
2 Bedroom
Granny Flat 60m²

FLOOR AREA
GROUND FLOOR LIVING   80.0 m2
FRONT VERANDAH   3.6 m2

TOTAL   83.6 m2

The Parramatta Granny Flat is our traditional standard design. Designed to be functional and a great use of space for the size. This design has been our most popular and the clients who have had this Granny Flat built on their land have all commented on the great size of the kitchen and living area and also the bedrooms which come with built in robes.

A STUDY - TYPICAL BRITISH HOUSES

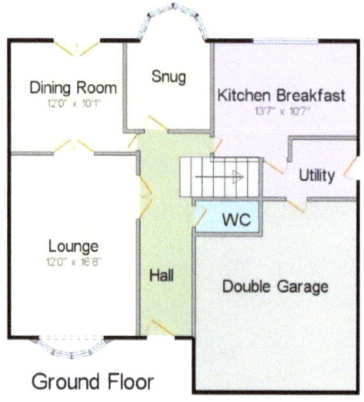

Ground Floor

1st Floor

HOUSE STUDY 1

Existing Layout

4 bedroom house typical executive style

Adequate but not huge spaces

A couple of interesting rooms downstairs but nothing extra upstairs

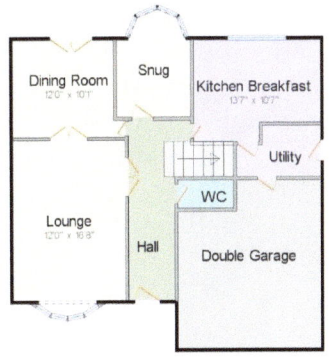

Ground Floor

1st Floor

granny flat is edged in blue

ALTERNATIVE PLAN B

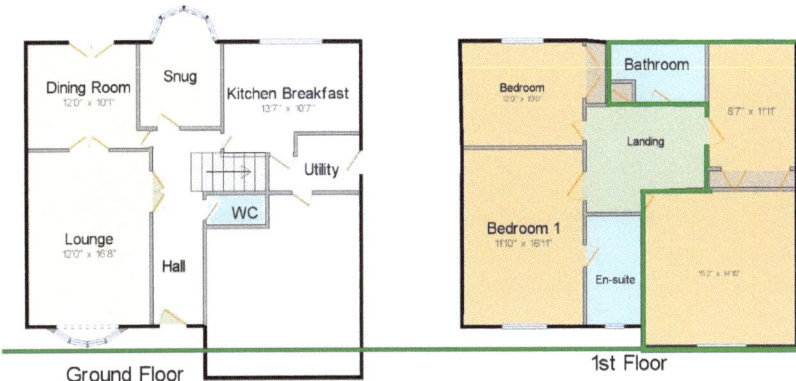

Ground Floor

1st Floor

THIS USES THE SAME ROOMS BUT TAKES THE EXISTING BATHROOM FOR THE GRANNY
FLAT = THE DOOR MAY NEED TO BE CHANGED AND AN ADDITIONAL EN SUITE WOULD
HAVE TO BE INSTALLED

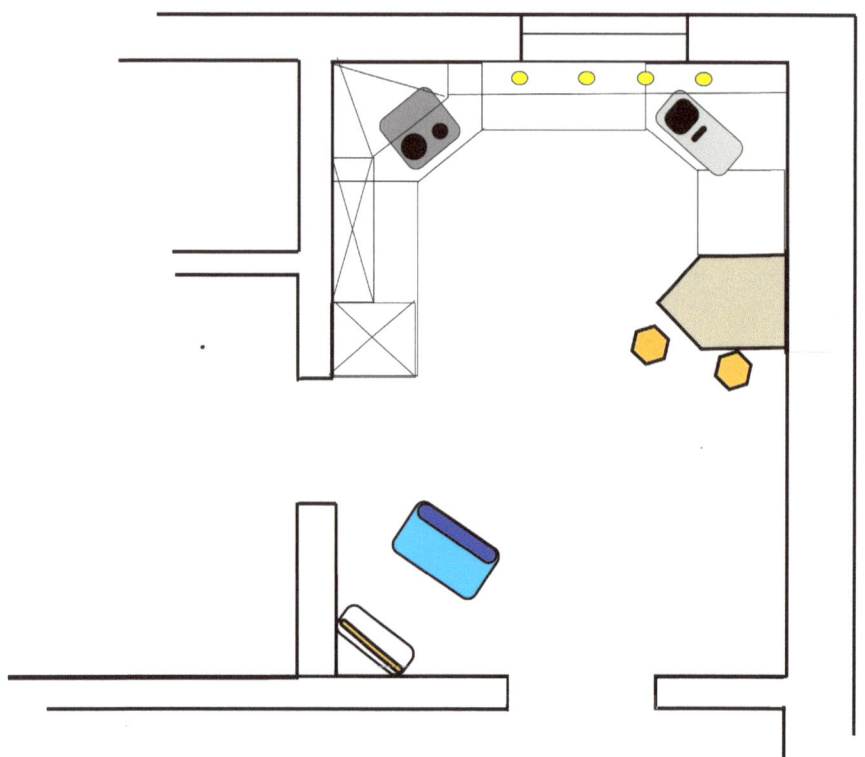

The area below will be the new bedroom with the bottom corner converted into a new en suite using the adjacent plumbing.

This plan is based upon Plan A, not using the existing bathroom but leaving that for the other bedrooms. Instead the larger area below this area will become the bedroom for the granny flat and a new en-suite built directly beside the existing en suite so plumbing would be simple. As this is a large bedroom there would be plenty of space and the kitchen diner would fit comfortably in the top room which will be the main entrance to the self contained flat

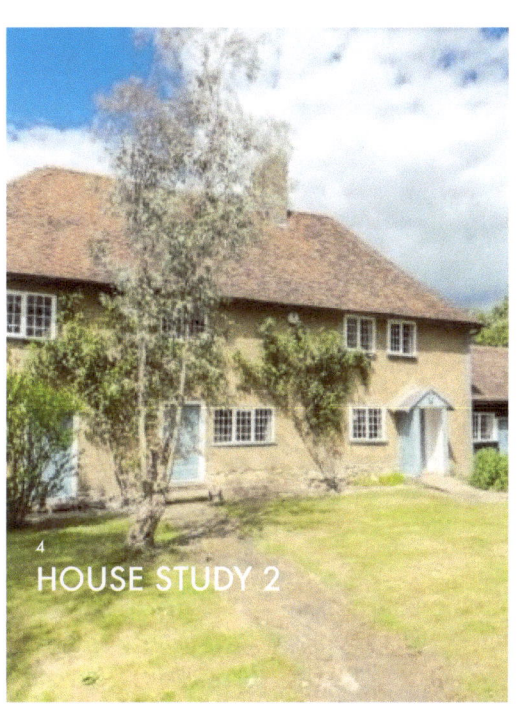

4
HOUSE STUDY 2

Ground Floor

MAIN FEATURES

HOUSE STUDY 2 FOR GRANNY FLAT CONVERSION

1. Interesting features e.g two staircases

2. Two building entrances

3. Existing annex

4. Large garage next to annex

5. Lots of odd rooms downstairs

6. What to do?

Ground Floor

Area outlined in red is the new granny flat with its own entrance and staircase - the area shown as annex also contains the shower room and the main entrance. The upstairs bedroom has an attached bathroom so the shower room could be removed but the annex which is now the living area could contain a sofa bed or fold down bed for guests?

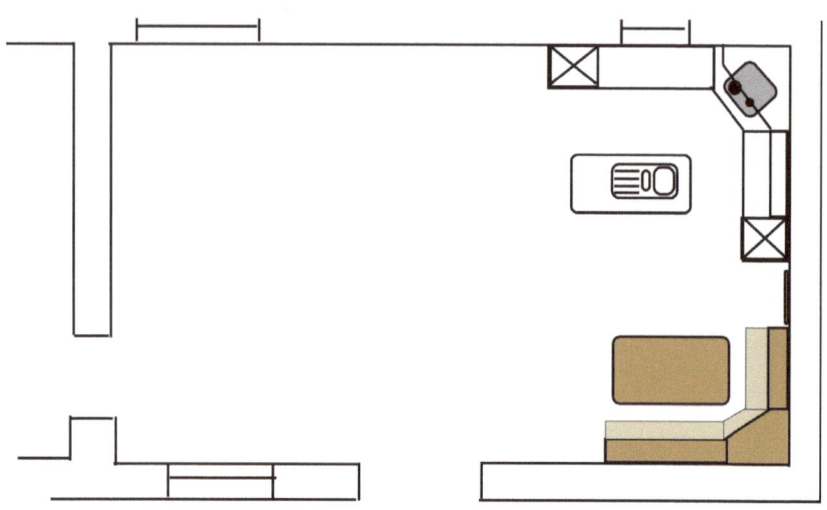

KITCHEN IN THE MAIN
ANNEX AREA

WE HAVE KEPT THE
KITCHEN DINER TO THE
ONE SIDE LEAVING A HUGE
AREA FOR LIVING .THE
DINING AREA

BOTTOM RIGHT IS A
CLASSIC GERMAN BENCH
DESIGN WITH STORAGE IN
THE UPPER BACKREST
SECTIONS SHOWN IN DARK
BROWN

5
HOUSE STUDY 3

Bedroom
12'8" x 9'6"

Bedroom
12'4" x 15'6"

Hall

Bathroo

Study
5' x 14'0"

Dining Room
15'7" x 8'5"

Kitchen Breakfast
13'1" x 26'7"

Sun Room

Family Room
14'6" x 16'2"

Lounge
12'7" x 15'9"

Garage
10'6" x 16'3"

Entrance Hall

Ground Floor

Landing

Shower Room

Bedroom
12'1" x 16'6"

Bedroom
12'5" x 9'6"

1st Floor

MAIN FEATURES

HOUSE 3

1. The first floor is tailor made to use as a granny flat

2. It may be necessary to install a chair lift or even a full size lift but this would not be a problem

3. Looking at the view of the property it would not be too difficult to install a dedicated entrance and stairs for the granny flat

Bedroom
9'7" x 18'6"

Landing

Shower Room

kitchen-dine-lounge

13'7" x 11'8"

1st Floor

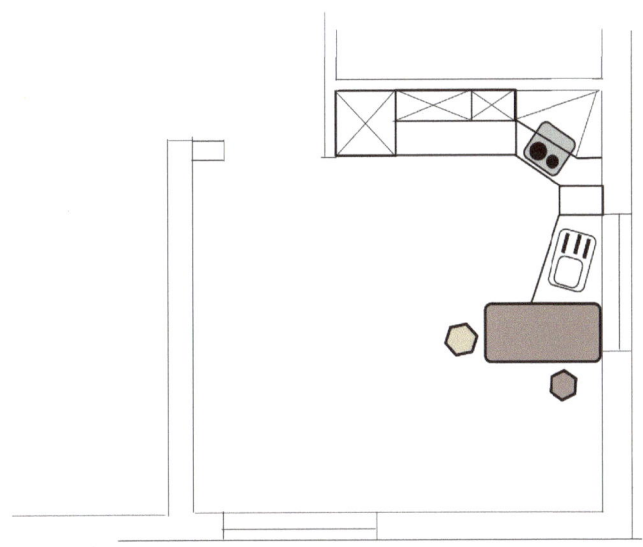

A REAL LIFE STUDY

OUR HOUSE CONVERTED TO GRANNY FLAT

• Budget was small

• Ground floor for Mum with bedroom and direct access to conservatory and nice large lounge

• All self contained with direct access to front door - which actually proved to be a problem as she kept on trying to walk back home which was over 200 miles away.

We moved into my mother's house when she turned 94. She was suffering from cerebral dementia and her health was failing fast. After a number of trips to the Hospital it was clear that this property was not suitable and we had to move. We gradually convinced her to move to a new property that would have the facilities we both needed

LEGEND

1.600 base for crockery

2.Liebherr fridge freezer

3.butcher trolley

4.500 cooker

5.450 dishwasher

6.600 sink unit

7.stainless steel bin

8.large stainless storage

9.microwave with TV

This plan rejected - too expensive

After moving to our new house Mum was finally taken ill again some 4 months later and died in hospital.

Our Granny flat arrangements had worked incredibly well and after beefing up the kitchen slightly we continued to use the new kitchen rather than the original one.

The facilities were frankly, excellent and all that was necessary was to install the large stainless steel commercial shelving unit that completed our storage.

7

OTHER GARDEN BUILDINGS

SUMMER HOUSES

Although the Granny Flat U.S. style hasn't really hit Europe yet there are still many other buildings placed in gardens and one of the very popular ones are Summer Houses. We are going to have a look at a range of these to see how suitable they are for conversion. Planning permission is easy.

The summer house example on the previous page is a very simple structure without the need for foundations. You should be able to get planning permission for this in any reasonable circumstances.

The top left example is about the same size but in this case would need foundations.

The bottom left is still around the same size but this looks like a little cottage and is just what Mum would like.

These examples are not much larger but they are certainly somewhat grander but apart from the cost would still be eminently suitable for conversion.

These examples are not much larger but they are certainly somewhat grander but apart from the cost would still be eminently suitable for conversion.

The construction of most of these examples is a simple wooden structure and often with no or very simple foundations. We have shown a variety of floor plans for these types of buildings

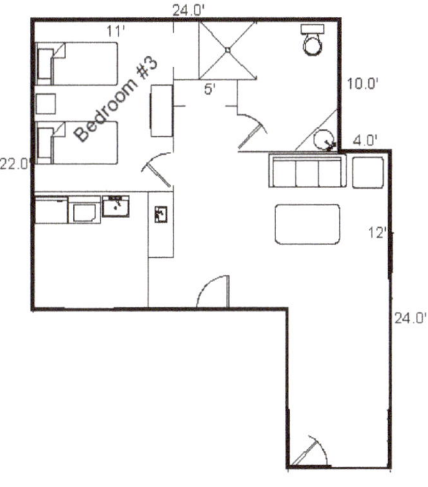

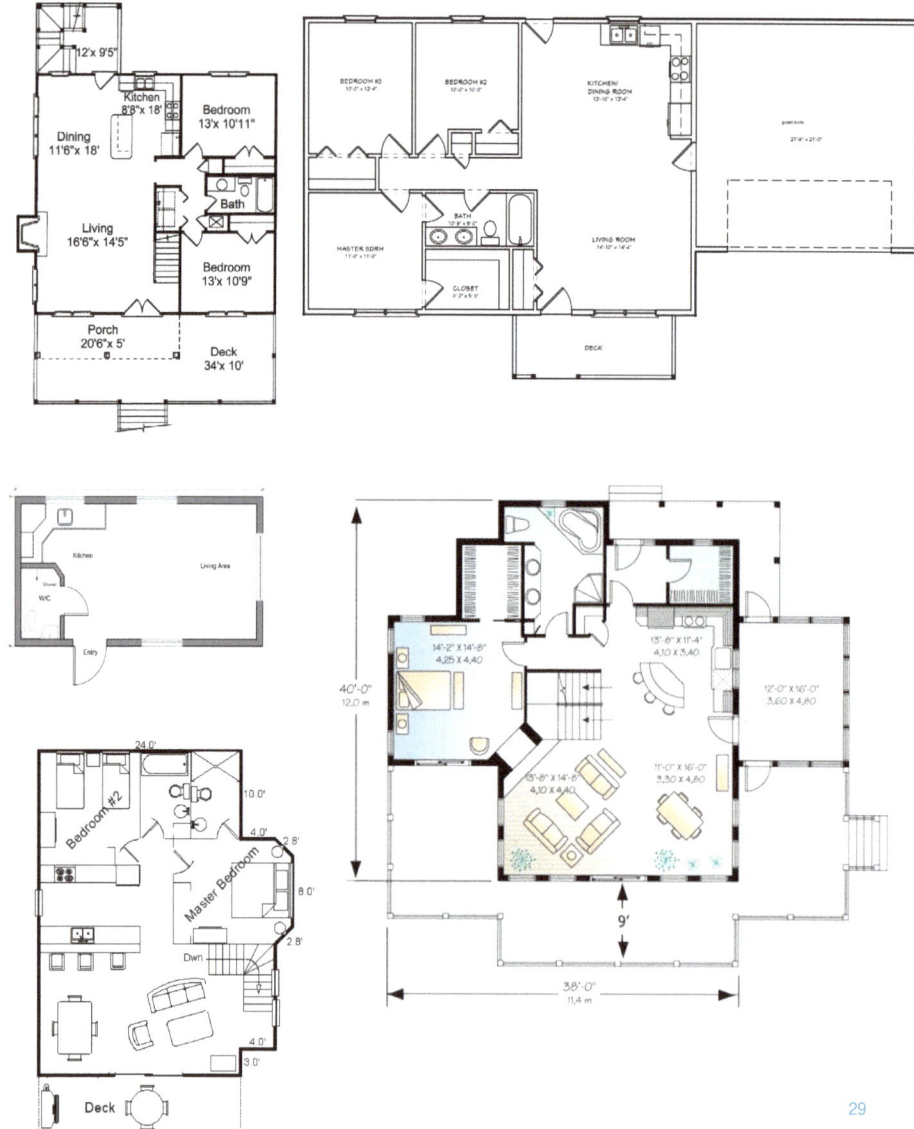

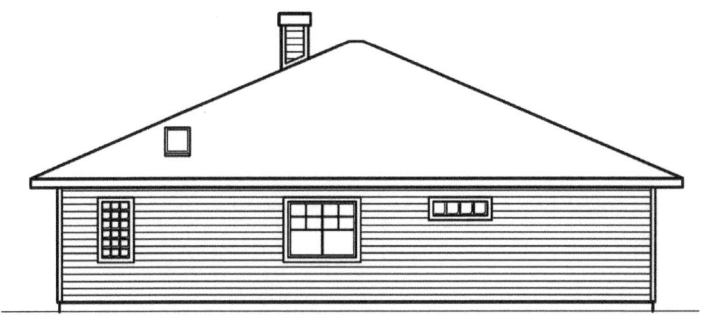

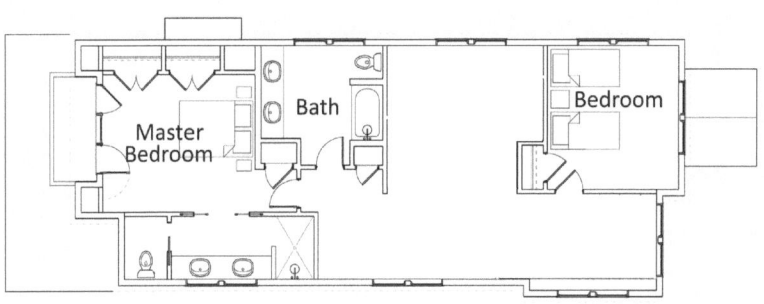

Master
Bedroom

Bath

Bedroom

The lounge has incorporated additional areas. The en suite with the master bed remains the same and the other bathroom has been left to serve guests and bedroom 2. Bathroom could be reduced in size to enlarge the lounge

Thank you for purchasing this latest version of our Mini guide.

We want you to enjoy this publication and learn from it,

To this end we offer TOTAL SUPPORT - if you feel you need help or clarification on any points or if you would like to receive a detailed exercise which you can submit for critique, please log in to our website at

www.kbb2000.com

KITCHEN PLANNING ESSENTIALS

I POINT PERSPECTIVE & VANISHING POINT

SURVEYING TECHNIQUES

EXTERIOR PRESENTATIONS

KITCHEN PLANNING APPLIANCES ESSENTIALS

2 POINT PERSPECTIVE & VANISHING POINT

GRANNY FLATS

CLOAK ROOMS DRESSING ROOMS CLOSETS

KITCHEN PLANING + DESIGN

BIRDS EYE PERSPECTIVE

KITCHEN WORKING TRIANGLE RULES

DOUBLE WORKING TRIANGLE

BATHROOM PLANNING

BEDROOM PRESENTATION

CREATIVE INTERIOR DESIGN USING A COMPUTER

CAD VS BRAIN

BATHROOM DESIGN

BATHROOM PRESENTATION

Avery C32011

Avery C32015

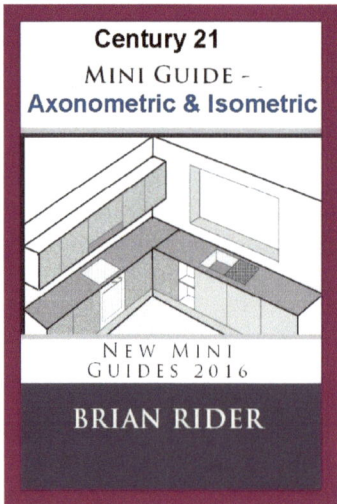

Century 21

MINI GUIDE -
Axonometric & Isometric

NEW MINI GUIDES 2016

BRIAN RIDER

Century 21

MINI GUIDE -
Kitchen   Planning

NEW MINI GUIDES 2016

BRIAN RIDER

www.ingramcontent.com/pod-product-compliance
Lightning Source LLC
Chambersburg PA
CBHW050907290526
45792CB00002B/727